CONNECT BIBLE STUDIES

John Grisham's Thrillers

Random House

The Lawyer
The Victim
The Criminal
The Judge

www.connectbiblestudies.com

connect
linking the Word to the world

CONNECT BIBLE STUDIES: John Grisham's Thrillers

Published in this format by Scripture Union, 207–209 Queensway, Bletchley, MK2 2EB, England.
Scripture Union is an international Christian charity working with churches in more than 130 countries providing resources to bring the good news about Jesus Christ to children, young people and families – and to encourage them to develop spiritually through the Bible and prayer. As well as a network of volunteers, staff and associates who run holidays, church-based events and school Christian groups, Scripture Union produces a wide range of publications and supports those who use the resources through training programmes.

Email: info@scriptureunion.org.uk
Internet: www.scriptureunion.org.uk

© Damaris Trust, PO Box 200, Southampton, SO17 2DL.
Damaris Trust enables people to relate Christian faith and contemporary culture. It helps them to think about issues within society from a Christian perspective and explore God's truth as it is revealed in the Bible. Damaris provides resources via the Internet, workshops, publications and products.
Email: office@damaris.org
Internet: www.damaris.org

British Library Cataloguing-in-Publication Data: a catalogue record for this book is available from the British Library.
First published 2003 ISBN 1 84427 021 1
All rights reserved. Generally, any part of this publication may only be reproduced or transmitted in any form or by any means with prior permission of the copyright holder. But purchasers of this set of Connect Bible Studies may print, photocopy or otherwise reproduce the Members Sheets for use in any group in which they are actively involved. In addition, the complete set may be printed or photocopied once for use in a single group.

ALSO AVAILABLE AS AN ELECTRONIC DOWNLOAD: www.connectbiblestudies.com

Damaris writers: Di Archer, Caroline Puntis, Tony Watkins, Steve Williams
SU editors: Lin Ball, Andrew Clark

Cover design by aricot vert of Fleet, UK.
Cover photos by kind permission of Random House.

Print production by CPO, Garcia Estate, Canterbury Road, Worthing, West Sussex BN13 1BW.
CPO is a Christian publishing charity working in partnership with over 30,000 churches and other Christian organisations worldwide, using the power of design and print to convey the message of Jesus Christ. Established for over 45 years, CPO is the UK's premier supplier of publicity and related resources to the UK Church, available through a direct mail catalogue series, an e-commerce website and most Christian bookshops.
Email:connect@cpo.org.uk
Internet:www.cpo-online.org

Other titles in this series:

Harry Potter and the Goblet of Fire 1 85999 578 0	**AI: Artificial Intelligence** 1 85999 626 4
The Matrix 1 85999 579 9	**Lord of the Rings** 1 85999 634 5
U2: All that you can't leave behind 1 85999 580 2	**The Simpsons** 1 85999 529 2
Billy Elliot 1 85999 581 0	**Iris** 1 85999 669 8
Chocolat 1 85999 608 6	**Dido: No Angel** 1 85999 679 5
TV Game Shows 1 85999 609 4	**Sven: On Football** 1 85999 690 6
How to be Good 1 85999 610 8	**Superheroes** 1 85999 702 3
Destiny's Child: 'Survivor' 1 85999 613 2	**The Pullman Trilogy** 1 85999 714 7
Friends 1 85999 775 9	**James Bond 007** 1 84427 007 6

And more titles following. Check www.connectbiblestudies.com for latest titles or ask at any good Christian bookshop.

connect

linking the Word to the world

Using Connect Bible Studies

What are these studies?

These innovative home group Bible studies have two aims. Firstly, to enable people to dig into their Bibles and get to know them better. Secondly, by being based on contemporary films, books, TV programmes etc, the aim is to help people think through topical issues in a Biblical way.

It is not envisaged that all the group will always be able to watch the films or read the books, or indeed that they will always want to. A summary is always provided. However, our vision is that knowing about these films and books empowers Christians engage with friends and colleagues about them. Addressing issues from a Biblical perspective gives Christians confidence that they know what they think, and can bring a distinctive angle to bear in conversations.

The studies are each produced with four weeks' worth of group material. These are available in print, published by Scripture Union, from your local Christian bookshop, or via the Internet at www.connectbiblestudies.com. Anyone can sign up for a free monthly email newsletter that announces the new studies and provides other information (sign up on the Connect Bible Studies website at www.connectbiblestudies.com/uk/register).

How do I use them?

Studies are designed to stimulate creative thought and discussion within a Biblical context. Each section has a range of questions or options from which the leader may choose in order to tailor the study to your group's needs and desires. Different approaches may appeal at different times, so the studies aim to supply choice.

Group members should all be supplied with the appropriate sheet to fill in – either by having their own copy of the booklet, or by having a photocopy of the Members' Sheet which follows each study session.

Leader's notes contain:

1. Opening questions

These help your group settle in to discussion, while introducing the topics. They may be straightforward, personal or creative, but aim to provoke a response.

2. Summary

We suggest the summary of the book or film will follow now, read aloud if necessary. There may well be reactions that group members want to express even before getting on to the week's issue.

3. Key issue

Again, either read from the leader's notes, or summarise.

4. Bible study

Lots of choice here. Choose as appropriate to suit your group – get digging into the Bible. Background reading and texts for further help and study are suggested, but please use the material provided to inspire your group to explore their Bibles as much as possible. A concordance might be a handy standby for looking things up. A commentary could be useful too, such as the New Bible Commentary 21st century edition (IVP, 1994). The idea is to help people to engage with the truth of God's word, wrestling with it if necessary but making it their own.

Don't plan to work through every question here. Within each section the two questions explore roughly the same ground but from different angles or in different ways. Our advice is to take one question from each section. The questions are open-ended so each ought to yield good discussion – though of course any discussion in a Bible study may need prompting to go a little further.

5. Implications

Here the aim is to tie together the perspectives gained through Bible study and the impact of the book or film. The implications may be personal, a change in worldview, or new ideas for relating to non-churchgoers. Choose questions that adapt to the flow of the discussion.

6. Prayer

Leave time for it! We suggest a time of open prayer, or praying in pairs if the group would prefer. Encourage your members to focus on issues from your study that had a particular impact on them. Try different approaches to prayer – light a candle, say a prayer each, write prayers down, play quiet worship music – aiming to facilitate everyone to relate to God.

7. Background reading

You will find links to some background reading on the Connect Bible Studies website: www.connectbiblestudies.com/

8. Online Discussion

You can discuss the studies online with others on the Connect Bible Studies website at www.connectbiblestudies.com/discuss/

Scriptures referred to are taken from the Holy Bible, New International Version (NIV). Copyright © 1973, 1978, 1984 by International Bible Society. Other Bible translations can, of course, be used for the studies and having a range of translations in a group can be helpful and useful in discussion.

connect

linking the Word to the world

John Grisham's Thrillers

Random House

Part One: The Lawyer

... once he had the attention of the courtroom, he gazed upon his potential jurors. These were his people ... This was his case, one he'd filed in his hometown so he could one day stand in this, his courtroom, and seek justice from his people.
The Runaway Jury, p25

Please read Using Connect Bible Studies *(page 3) before leading a Bible study with this material.*

Opening Questions

Choose one of these questions.

Do you like Grisham's thrillers? Why/why not?	Would you make a good lawyer? Why/why not?
Why do you think courtroom dramas are so popular?	What law would you like to change or create and why?

Summary

In the thick of a John Grisham bestseller, you may often find yourself enjoying the thrill of a dramatic courtroom scene. This is the playground of lawyers – there is never a shortage of excitement because the stakes are always high. In *The Runaway Jury* the entire tobacco industry goes on trial in what is set to be a landmark case in the history of civil law. The lawyers bombard the jury with testimonies and evidence as they wrestle with the issue of legal responsibility – can the cigarette companies be blamed for the death of the plaintiff's husband, a heavy smoker?

For young law student Darby Shaw in *The Pelican Brief,* evidence is paramount. In response to the murders of two High Court judges, Darby sets out to find a link that will lead her to the killer. Unfortunately, the implications of her brief reach as far as the White House. When her theory ends up in the wrong hands, Darby becomes the chief witness and finds herself on the run. With the help of influential journalist Gray Grantham, Darby uses her quick wits and knowledge of the law to keep one step ahead of her pursuers.

In matters of criminal law, the lawyer has a duty to construct the best possible defence on behalf of the defendant, guilty or not. Occasionally, as Jake Tyler Brigance finds in *A Time to Kill*, the right verdict may prove to be elusive – defending a black man in the Deep South on trial for murder is a grey area. Jake's mentor, Lucien Wilbanks, sums it up: 'If you win this case, justice will prevail, and if you lose, justice will also prevail. Now that is a strange case.'

Key Issue: The Lawyer

The lawyer is often a key figure in Grisham's stories. While he, or she, usually represents a client with flair and skill, the lawyer is not immune to financial, moral or personal pressure. Although this gives Grisham fiction much of its exciting edge, it also begs the question: what value does the law really have? Our study asks what the Bible has to say about law, how it views the importance of evidence, and why we all need an advocate. Finally, we look at Jesus and the law.

Bible Study

Choose one question from each section.

1. Law

> *On one side of the bar were two hundred little people, those dragged into court by the power of the law. On the other side was the law itself – the Judge sitting elevated above the rest, the packs of stuffy lawyers looking down their nasty noses, the clerks, the deputies, the bailiffs.* (The Runaway Jury, p29)

◆ Read Exodus 20:1–21. Why did God give the law? In what ways would the law shape society? On what was the law based?

Leaders: Western law codes are partly based on the Ten Commandments and other principles derived from the Law of Moses found in the first five books of the Bible. The law was designed to enable Israel to maintain their covenant relationship with God.

◆ Read Galatians 3:10–25 and 1 Timothy 1:8–10. What does the law do? What does the law not do?

2. Evidence

I checked with all my sources last night at the Bureau, at Langley, the White House. All of them said the brief doesn't exist – never has. You may be the only witness that can ever prove there was a brief. If you disappear, so does justice. (Gray Grantham, *The Pelican Brief*, dir. Alan J. Pakula, 1993)

◆ Read Deuteronomy 19:15–21. How is the character of God reflected in this passage? How important is evidence?

◆ Read Acts 24:1–23. What case did Tertullus bring against Paul? How did Paul defend himself? What was his main concern?

3. Advocate

You wanted this case, well you got it. It isn't easy saving the world, even one case at a time, but you stick with it. (Lucien Wilbanks, *A Time to Kill*, dir. Joel Schumacher, 1996)

◆ Read Genesis 18:16–33. How did Abraham present his case? Why did God listen to Abraham?

◆ Read 2 Samuel 14:1–24. How did the woman from Tekoa present her case? Why did David listen to the woman?

Leaders: The background to this incident is in the previous chapter. David's first son, Amnon, raped his half-sister Tamar. Her brother Absalom (David's third son) bided his time for two years before arranging to have Amnon killed in revenge. Afterwards he fled from his father until Joab judged the time to be right for bringing about some kind of reconciliation.

4. Jesus and the law

In all this legal manoeuvring, something has gotten lost. And that something is the truth. It is incumbent upon us lawyers not to just talk about the truth, but to actually seek it, to find it, to live it. (Jake Tyler Brigance, *A Time to Kill*, dir. Joel Schumacher, 1996)

◆ Read Matthew 5:17–20. What is Jesus' perspective on the law? In what sense does he fulfil it?

Leaders: Jesus contrasts fulfilling the law with abolishing it. But here Jesus is not just talking about perfectly meeting the requirements of the law. Matthew always uses the word 'fulfil' to refer to fulfilled prophecy. Jesus is the fulfilment of 'the Law and the Prophets' (a phrase meaning the entire Old Testament) because they point forward to him and anticipate the kingdom of God which he came to usher in.

◆ Read Hebrews 7:11–28 and 1 John 2:1. What is the ultimate weakness of the law? Why is Jesus a unique advocate for us before God?

Implications

You're an attorney, be proud. Your job is to find Justice, no matter how well she may hide herself from you. (Lucien Wilbanks, *A Time to Kill*, dir. Joel Schumacher, 1996)

Choose one or more of the following questions.

- ◆ We live in a 'pick and mix' society where rules are not welcomed. What is your personal concept of right and wrong based on? What is society's?

- ◆ Is it possible to divide law from God?

- ◆ If truth matters to God, are there things you have hidden from him or others which you need to confess?

- ◆ Do you stand up for yourself and other people in trouble? How could God help you in this?

- ◆ What does it mean to you that Jesus died to set you free from the condemnation of the law? How does this affect the way you live?

- ◆ In what ways does the law as given in the Ten Commandments challenge you? What difference does Jesus make?

- ◆ What would you say to a friend who thinks he doesn't have to bother with the law 'as long as I don't hurt anybody'?

Prayer

Spend some time praying through these issues.

Background Reading

You will find links to some background reading on the Connect Bible Studies website: www.connectbiblestudies.com/uk/catalogue/0019/background.htm

Discuss

Discuss this study in the online discussion forums at www.connectbiblestudies.com/discuss

Members' Sheet: John Grisham's Thrillers – Part 1
Summary

In the thick of a John Grisham bestseller, you may often find yourself enjoying the thrill of a dramatic courtroom scene. This is the playground of lawyers – there is never a shortage of excitement because the stakes are always high. In *The Runaway Jury* the entire tobacco industry goes on trial in what is set to be a landmark case in the history of civil law. The lawyers bombard the jury with testimonies and evidence as they wrestle with the issue of legal responsibility – can the cigarette companies be blamed for the death of the plaintiff's husband, a heavy smoker?

For young law student Darby Shaw in *The Pelican Brief,* evidence is paramount. In response to the murders of two High Court judges, Darby sets out to find a link that will lead her to the killer. Unfortunately, the implications of her brief reach as far as the White House. When her theory ends up in the wrong hands, Darby becomes the chief witness and finds herself on the run. With the help of influential journalist Gray Grantham, Darby uses her quick wits and knowledge of the law to keep one step ahead of her pursuers.

In matters of criminal law, the lawyer has a duty to construct the best possible defence on behalf of the defendant, guilty or not. Occasionally, as Jake Tyler Brigance finds in *A Time to Kill,* the right verdict may prove to be elusive – defending a black man in the Deep South on trial for murder is a grey area. Jake's mentor, Lucien Wilbanks, sums it up: 'If you win this case, justice will prevail, and if you lose, justice will also prevail. Now that is a strange case.'

Key Issue

Bible Study notes

Implications

Prayer

www.connectbiblestudies.com

connect
linking the Word to the world

John Grisham's Thrillers

Random House

Part Two: The Victim

'How's your head?'
'No additional brain damage.'
'How's your soul?'
'Tortured to say the least. But I'll survive.'
The King of Torts, pp367,368

Please read Using Connect Bible Studies *(page 3) before leading a Bible study with this material.*

Opening Questions

Choose one of these questions.

Why do bad things happen to good people?	Why do we usually feel sorry for victims?
Have you been a victim of a crime? How did you feel?	How strongly do you feel about your rights?

Summary

John Grisham's characters frequently have a twist – a criminal who is also a victim; a good lawyer corrupted by the prospect of power. In the Deep South, the backdrop for *A Time to Kill*, emotions are running high. The tension between the white and black communities has reached breaking point. When a group of white boys terrorise and rape a young black girl, her father loses his head and shoots the perpetrators. But as lawyer Jake Tyler Brigance points out, before Carl Lee Hailey became a murderer he was a victim. On the one hand, the full force of the law is against him; on the other, he has rights. The question is, will his rights prove him wrong?

In the world of mass tort litigation described in *The King of Torts*, there is always a victim who needs to be compensated. One woman's son was shot by a deranged boy who was affected by untested drugs. A whole community lives in houses which are crumbling because of a bad batch of cement. As lawyer Clay Carter discovers, where there's a victim, there's a huge pile of cash in compensation. The right man can make a killing on his clients' pain and distress, and go away with a relatively clear conscience. When the roller coaster reaches the top of the ride, Clay unwittingly becomes the victim of his own greed. The people he once sought to compensate now feel that he has double-crossed them. As his own life is threatened, Clay experiences the perilous ride down.

Key Issue: The Victim

Perhaps of all Grisham's characters, the victim is the easiest to identify with. Our compassion and outrage are readily aroused when someone is injured by another, whether the perpetrator is a multinational company or a mugger. We have an instinctive reaction that something should be done to put things right. So what is the Bible's attitude towards victims? Does it agree that a victim has been wronged? Does a victim have rights, and is the fight for compensation justified? Does Jesus understand?

Bible Study

Choose one question from each section.

1. Wronged

As Adelfa Pumphrey sat at her desk with her face in her hands, she thought of her son and his lifeless body lying somewhere in the city at that moment ... She swore revenge on whoever killed him. She cursed his father for abandoning the child. She cried for her baby. And she knew she would survive. Somehow, she would survive.
(The King of Torts, p3,4)

◆ Read 1 Kings 21:1–16. In what ways was Naboth wronged? What were the wrongdoers' motives?

Leaders: Land was a vital issue for Israel. When they entered the Promised Land, it was distributed to the Israelite families by lot to be their inheritance (see Deuteronomy 26:53). Keeping the land in the family, therefore, was seen as equivalent to keeping a share in Israel's inheritance of the land as a whole. The day of fasting (v. 9) was meant to suggest that some serious sin had been committed and action needed to be taken.

◆ Read Psalm 35:1–28. How had David been wronged? How did David deal with his pain?

2. Rights

I set out to prove a black man could receive a fair trial in the South, that we are all equal in the eyes of the law. That's not the truth, because the eyes of the law are human eyes – yours and mine – and until we can see each other as equals, justice is never going to be even-handed. (Jake Tyler Brigance, *A Time to Kill*, dir. Joel Schumacher, 1996)

◆ Read Exodus 21:12–25. Why were rights necessary? Whose rights did this part of the law safeguard and how?

Leaders: The principle of the compensation matching the crime (verses 23–25) is called the Lex Talionis (law of retaliation). It both restricted the damages someone could expect and prevented personal vendettas. With this law, retaliation was limited and just – rather than being allowed to escalate. See also Matthew 5:38–48 where Jesus goes further to say that even justifiable retribution is not appropriate within the kingdom of God.

◆ Read Acts 22:21–29; 25:7–12. How were Paul's rights abused? What happened when Paul insisted on his rights?

Leaders: Although Paul stood on his rights at these points, he did not always think it appropriate. See 1 Corinthians 9:1–18, where Paul explains why he did not use his rights as an apostle, so that the good news of Jesus Christ was not hindered in any way.

3. Compensation

'If you want the money, sign right there.'
'I feel like I'm doing something wrong,' she said at one point.
'No, the wrong has been done by someone else. You're the victim here, Adelfa, the victim and now the client.' (*The King of Torts,* p110)

◆ Read Exodus 22:1–15. What does this passage say about restitution? How is restitution balanced with the wrong committed?

◆ Read Luke 19:1–10. What was extraordinary about Zacchaeus' response to Jesus? Why did Jesus declare him to be a 'son of Abraham'?

Leaders: Jesus' contemporaries excluded tax collectors because they collaborated with the occupying Roman army and also extorted extra money out of the people. To understand how generous Zacchaeus was in his response to Jesus, see Numbers 5:7.

4. Jesus the willing victim

Throughout the long night, Clay drowned in self-pity – his badly bruised ego; the utter humiliation among peers, friends, and employees; the delight of his enemies; the dread of tomorrow and the public flogging he would take in the press, with no one to defend him. (*The King of Torts,* p295)

◆ Read Isaiah 53:1–12. How did the people react to the victim and his suffering? What did they fail to see? In what ways does Jesus fulfil this prophecy?

◆ Read Matthew 26:59–68; 27:12–14, 26–40. List the things that were done to Jesus, and the things that Jesus did. In what ways was he a victim? In what ways was he still in control?

Leaders: Jesus had been betrayed by one of his small group of committed disciples, arrested at night, and tried by the Sanhedrin (Jewish ruling council) although it was illegal for this to happen at night and in less than two days.

Implications

The survivors of dead people out there were actually suing and asking for huge sums of money because cigarettes cause lung cancer, they claimed. (*The Runaway Jury,* p12)

Choose one or more of the following questions.

◆ Is anger on behalf of victims – whether yourself or others – justified? Where could it lead?

◆ When should we stand up for our own or others' rights? When should we hold back?

◆ Christians are often passionate about helping all sorts of victims. As a group, share what you are doing to help others. How could you encourage and inspire one another in this?

◆ Have you been a victim in the past, or do you feel victimised at the moment? Are there issues you need to deal with? How could God, and your group, help you?

◆ How does our trust in God relate to the fight or desire for compensation?

◆ Is there anyone you need to make amends to?

◆ What would you say to a friend who thinks Jesus was just a good man who died young?

Prayer

Spend some time praying through these issues.

Background Reading

You will find links to some background reading on the Connect Bible Studies website: www.connectbiblestudies.com/uk/catalogue/0019/background.htm

Discuss

Discuss this study in the online discussion forums at www.connectbiblestudies.com/discuss

Members' Sheet: John Grisham's Thrillers – Part 2

Summary

John Grisham's characters frequently have a twist – a criminal who is also a victim; a good lawyer corrupted by the prospect of power. In the Deep South, the backdrop for *A Time to Kill*, emotions are running high. The tension between the white and black communities has reached breaking point. When a group of white boys terrorise and rape a young black girl, her father loses his head and shoots the perpetrators. But as lawyer Jake Tyler Brigance points out, before Carl Lee Hailey became a murderer he was a victim. On the one hand, the full force of the law is against him; on the other, he has rights. The question is, will his rights prove him wrong?

In the world of mass tort litigation described in *The King of Torts*, there is always a victim who needs to be compensated. One woman's son was shot by a deranged boy who was affected by untested drugs. A whole community live in houses which are crumbling because of a bad batch of cement. As lawyer Clay Carter discovers, where there's a victim, there's a huge pile of cash in compensation. The right man can make a killing on his clients' pain and distress, and go away with a relatively clear conscience. When the roller coaster reaches the top of the ride, Clay unwittingly becomes the victim of his own greed. The people he once sought to compensate now feel that he has double-crossed them. As his own life is threatened, Clay experiences the perilous ride down.

Key Issue

Bible Study notes

Implications

Prayer

John Grisham's Thrillers

Random House

Part Three: The Criminal

This is a man who is a confessed murderer. This is a man who admitted on this stand to carrying out the sentences that he believed the alleged rapists of his daughter deserved. He's taken justice out of your hands [picks up a gun] and put it in his own. With those hands, he took the lives of two young men. We feel terrible about what happened to his daughter – but feeling terrible and knowing something is wrong does not give any of us a right to kill.
D.A. Rufus Buckley, *A Time to Kill,* dir. Joel Schumacher, 1996

Please read Using Connect Bible Studies *(page 3) before leading a Bible study with this material.*

Opening Questions

Choose one of these questions.

Do you ever hope the criminal in stories will get away with his crime? Why?	What is the worst crime?
Does crime really pay?	Why do people break the law?

Summary

If there is a dark underworld in the law profession, John Grisham certainly has the measure of it. For all the obvious criminals he conjures up, there is also a queue of suspicious-looking lawyers who deserve to be sent down. Most of his characters are not beyond corruption, particularly when there are large amounts of money involved. It is one small step from knowing how to work within the boundaries of the law to using it for criminal gain.

In *The King of Torts*, Clay Carter begins his career defending poor criminals for the Office of the Public Defender. One day he is offered a large amount of money to drop a case. His client is an ex-drug addict who randomly shot another youth when he was released from rehab. It emerges that the anti-addiction drug he was taking has had a curious effect – the desire to kill. The stranger who informs Clay is reluctant to name his employer, the company who produced the lethal drug. They want to sweep their mistake under the carpet, and have chosen Clay to do their dirty work. Deep down Clay knows that paying people off and making a profit is dubious, but he continues to take on more cases from the mysterious stranger. Victims across the country put their trust in Clay Carter, believing that he will win compensation on their behalf – in spite of the money he will cream off the top. It is not long before the stranger leads Clay onto the other side of the law, where the FBI is waiting for him.

Key Issue: The Criminal

It is not just the obvious baddies who qualify as criminals in Grisham's world. Respectable leaders and companies can get tempted into criminal activity too. But the law is there to hound them down and reveal their transgressions, and the Grisham criminal is likely to get his comeuppance. What does the Bible say about breaking the law, and the inevitable deception that goes along with it? Does it let criminals off the hook? What was Jesus' attitude to being treated as a criminal?

Bible Study

Choose one question from each section.

1. Lawbreaker

Those new at the mass tort game look often over their shoulders, as if what they're doing should somehow be illegal. With time, though, their hides grow so thick they think of themselves as Teflon. Clay jumped at the mere mention of the 'FBI', then chuckled at his own cowardice. He'd certainly done nothing wrong. (*The King of Torts*, p281)

◆ Read 1 Samuel 15:1–26. What command did Saul disobey? Why did Samuel take this law-breaking so seriously?

Leaders: The Amalekites were the first people to attack Israel and made their first targets the old and weak (Deuteronomy 25:17–19). They were deeply opposed to God and his people, and God had promised Moses that their memory would one day be completely obliterated (Exodus 17:14).

◆ Read Romans 2:17–29. According to Paul, what were the limitations of relying solely on the law? How could his readers avoid being law-breakers?

Leaders: The Jews saw their relationship with God in terms of keeping the Old Testament law. They were proud of the law and believed that it gave them moral superiority over Gentiles. They were also proud of being circumcised – the physical mark that they were members of God's special people.

2. Dishonest

Just make the money. It's a racket. It has nothing to do with being a lawyer. Find 'em, sign 'em, settle 'em, take the money and run. (*The King of Torts*, p262)

◆ Read Joshua 7:1–26. What did Joshua say was at stake because of the dishonesty? How did Achan's sin impact himself and the tribe?

◆ Read John 12:1-8; Mark 14:10–21. In what ways did Judas act dishonestly? How did Jesus prepare himself and the disciples for the consequences?

3. Punished

The monetary value of Jacob Wood's life was, say, a million dollars. He added in some other damages and the total became two million. These were actual damages, monetary amounts the family was entitled to because of Jacob's death.
But the case wasn't about actual damages. Rohr delivered a mini-lecture on punitive damages and their role in keeping corporate America in line. How do you punish a company that has eight hundred million dollars in cash? (*The Runaway Jury*, p436)

◆ Read Hosea 4:1–9. What was the charge God brought against the Israelites? How were they experiencing God's punishment?

◆ Read Romans 1:18–32. Why is God angry with mankind? What does God's punishment look like?

4. Jesus the criminal?

If you was on that jury, what would it take to convince you to set me free? (Carl Lee Hailey, *A Time to Kill*, dir. Joel Schumacher, 1996)

◆ Read Luke 23:1–43. Summarise the evidence for and against Jesus. What were the respective attitudes of each condemned man?

◆ Read 2 Corinthians 5:21 and 1 Peter 2:20–25. How was Jesus made into a criminal on our behalf? What difference does this make to us?

Implications

Mass tort litigation was not practising law. It was a roguish form of entrepreneurship.
(*The King of Torts,* p233)

Choose one or more of the following questions.

◆ What does it mean to you that obeying the law cannot save you – that you need Jesus?

◆ Do you grade sins? Does God? What law-breaking do you allow in your own life, and how could that change?

◆ Are you ever dishonest? How can you stop?

◆ How do you react to dishonesty or betrayal in others? How can God help you?

◆ What is the balance between receiving forgiveness from God, and having to live with the consequences of our actions?

◆ Jesus was treated like a criminal for us. How would you explain this to a neighbour who has never been to church?

◆ What would you say to someone who thinks any crime is OK as long as you don't get caught?

Prayer

Spend some time praying through these issues.

Background Reading

You will find links to some background reading on the Connect Bible Studies website:
www.connectbiblestudies.com/uk/catalogue/0019/background.htm

Discuss

Discuss this study in the online discussion forums at www.connectbiblestudies.com/discuss

Members' Sheet: John Grisham's Thrillers – Part 3

Summary

If there is a dark underworld in the law profession, John Grisham certainly has the measure of it. For all the obvious criminals he conjures up, there is also a queue of suspicious-looking lawyers who deserve to be sent down. Most of his characters are not beyond corruption, particularly when there are large amounts of money involved. It is one small step from knowing how to work within the boundaries of the law to using it for criminal gain.

In *The King of Torts*, Clay Carter begins his career defending poor criminals for the Office of the Public Defender. One day he is offered a large amount of money to drop a case. His client is an ex-drug addict who randomly shot another youth when he was released from rehab. It emerges that the anti-addiction drug he was taking has had a curious effect – the desire to kill. The stranger who informs Clay is reluctant to name his employer, the company who produced the lethal drug. They want to sweep their mistake under the carpet, and have chosen Clay to do their dirty work. Deep down Clay knows that paying people off and making a profit is dubious, but he continues to take on more cases from the mysterious stranger. Victims across the country put their trust in Clay Carter, believing that he will win compensation on their behalf – in spite of the money he will cream off the top. It is not long before the stranger leads Clay onto the other side of the law, where the FBI is waiting for him.

Key Issue

Bible Study notes

Implications

Prayer

connect

linking the Word to the world

John Grisham's Thrillers

Random House

Part Four: The Judge

'I have been informed that the jury has reached a verdict,' Harkin said loudly into his microphone, and he could see the lawyers shaking.
'Please bring in the jury.'
The Runaway Jury, p470

Please read Using Connect Bible Studies *(page 3) before leading a Bible study with this material.*

Opening Questions

Choose one of these questions.

What do you think of the way Grisham presents the American legal system?	Would you like to be a judge? Why/why not?
Some people are very judgmental. Why don't we like this?	Should we judge one another? Why/why not?

Summary

In the courtroom, there is only one final word and that belongs to the judge. He may deliver a verdict according to the wishes of his twelve jurors, but throughout the proceedings he is always in charge.

In *The Runaway Jury*, Judge Harkin presides over a particularly difficult case. Eight lawyers have got together to file a case against a tobacco company, one of the Big Four. The plaintiff is a woman who lost her husband to lung cancer. He was a heavy smoker – as far as she is concerned, smoking killed him. The tobacco companies know that if a big verdict is delivered against them, the doors will be opened to countless 'victims' suing on behalf of dead relatives.

Judge Harkin manages to control things in the courtroom, but behind the scenes a war is raging without his knowledge. The Big Four have hired an expert called Rankin Fitch to handle the case. He has chosen the defence lawyers and is secretly working on ways to get the verdict they require from the jury. He is prepared to use any means necessary, above or below board. When he takes steps to interfere with a member of the jury, the judge hauls counsel into his office. Both sides are convinced they are innocent. Fred Harkin makes it clear that he will not tolerate such behaviour. If it transpires that the proceedings are not being run fairly, there could be a mistrial. Judge Harkin is keen to protect his jury and is determined that conditions will favour the true course of justice.

Key Issue: The Judge

The judge is always a powerful figure in Grisham fiction. The judge influences juries, worries lawyers and directs the course of hard-won justice. As the stories race to a close, it is often the judge who has the last word. This reflects the overall sense of justice being done at the end of a Grisham story. In the truth of the Bible, what does it mean that God is the ultimate judge? Is God impartial? What are his decisions? What difference does Jesus make?

Bible Study

Choose one question from each section. You may like to follow the Ezekiel questions throughout.

1. Justice

'Uh, gee, Judge ... I'm certain we've done nothing wrong.' (Wendall Rohr, *The Runaway Jury*, p161)

◆ Read Ezekiel 20:1–12. Why does God judge? What does God want for his people? Why are the people left with no defence?

◆ Read Psalm 98:4–9; 2 Thessalonians 1:1–10. Why do people need God's justice? How should we prepare for his judgment?

2. Fairness

We have a duty under God to see the truth, not with our eyes and not with our minds – where fear and hate turn commonality into prejudice – but with our hearts, where we don't know better. (Jake Tyler Brigance, *A Time to Kill*, dir. Joel Schumacher, 1996)

◆ Read Ezekiel 18:1–20. What is the significance of God rejecting the proverb (v. 2)? How does God's justice work?

Leaders: The people were complaining that they were being punished because of earlier generations' wickedness – something they had drawn from Exodus 20:5. However, they misunderstood this principle. It is not that God punishes children for their parents' sin, rather that this sin deeply affects them and is likely to make them sinful in the same way. You may like to compare the actions Ezekiel describes with Exodus 20:1–17.

◆ Read Romans 2:1–11. In what ways is God fair? What are the implications of this for us?

3. The last word …

Any more of that nonsense, and you're all out of here! (Judge Omar Noose, *A Time to Kill*, dir. Joel Schumacher, 1996)

◆ Read Ezekiel 7:1–14. How does God respond to people's choices? In what way and why does God have the last word?

Leaders: The 'unheard-of disaster' (v. 5) is the catastrophic judgment of God on his own chosen people. The end of the nation seems to be imminent.

◆ Read Revelation 20:11–21:8. What picture of God does John get in his vision? What is God's last word on everything and everyone?

4. Jesus the judge

Assembled at this moment in his courtroom were some of the brightest legal minds and largest egos in the country. Fred Harkin was determined to rule with a heavy hand. (*The Runaway Jury*, p27)

◆ Read Ezekiel 1:25–28; 34:17–31. What kind of judge is God? How do these passages point forward to Jesus?

See also John 10:7-16; Revelation 1:12-20.

◆ Read John 7:53–8:20. Who is passing judgment on whom? What do we learn from these incidents about Jesus the judge?

Implications

With everyone on his side of the courtroom officially introduced, Rohr gave his brief summary of the case, a recitation that attracted immense interest from the defense lawyers and the Judge. They seemed ready to pounce if Rohr stepped over the invisible barrier between fact and argument. He didn't, but he enjoyed tormenting them. (The Runaway Jury, p41)

Choose one or more of the following questions.

- ◆ How does God as judge fit with his grace and mercy?

- ◆ How much is culture, background etc., responsible for how we are, and how much is our own choice?

- ◆ Do you find yourself blaming others for your own mistakes and problems? How could taking responsibility for yourself help you to grow?

- ◆ Does God have the right to judge your life? If so, what does this mean for you?

- ◆ What would you say to someone who says that surely God is too loving to judge anyone?

- ◆ Do you treat other people fairly, by God's standards?

- ◆ Do you really believe that God will judge the world in the end? What difference does that make to the way you live?

- ◆ Would you agree with a friend who thinks Grisham has a good sense of justice? Why/why not?

Prayer

Spend some time praying through these issues.

Background Reading

You will find links to some background reading on the Connect Bible Studies website: www.connectbiblestudies.com/uk/catalogue/0019/background.htm

Discuss

Discuss this study in the online discussion forums at www.connectbiblestudies.com/discuss

Summary

In the courtroom, there is only one final word and that belongs to the judge. He may deliver a verdict according to the wishes of his twelve jurors, but throughout the proceedings he is always in charge.

In *The Runaway Jury*, Judge Harkin presides over a particularly difficult case. Eight lawyers have got together to file a case against a tobacco company, one of the Big Four. The plaintiff is a woman who lost her husband to lung cancer. He was a heavy smoker – as far as she is concerned, smoking killed him. The tobacco companies know that if a big verdict is delivered against them, the doors will be opened to countless 'victims' suing on behalf of dead relatives.

Judge Harkin manages to control things in the courtroom, but behind the scenes a war is raging without his knowledge. The Big Four have hired an expert called Rankin Fitch to handle the case. He has chosen the defence lawyers and is secretly working on ways to get the verdict they require from the jury. He is prepared to use any means necessary, above or below board. When he takes steps to interfere with a member of the jury, the judge hauls counsel into his office. Both sides are convinced they are innocent. Fred Harkin makes it clear that he will not tolerate such behaviour. If it transpires that the proceedings are not being run fairly, there could be a mistrial. Judge Harkin is keen to protect his jury and is determined that conditions will favour the true course of justice.

Key Issue

Bible Study notes

Implications

Prayer